This 2 is Love

This 2 is Love

A Spoken Word Joint

By

Rudwaan

copyright © 2013
all rights reserved

no portion of this work
may be reproduced or used
in any form for profit or gain
without the author's prior
expressed and explicit consent

Author: Rudwaan
Publisher: Move The Village

edit and format by
Rudwaan

manuscript prep by
Terri Mimms

cover design by
Arlin James Swanson
3e4me.com

ISBN 978-0-9900279-0-4

CONTENTS

Livications
Pre-word
Nothing but Love here 1
Let us Love them 2
This 2 is Love 5
Love Exposed 8
Heart beats the Drum 10
Stirred not Shaken 13
After the Storm 15
Girl, don't you know? 16
Think Supreme 20
Forgiveness is a Process 22
Sister, forgive me 23
Django Unchained 28
Tis their season 31
Two Dreams Dreaming 34
Be here 36
The Wanting 37
Ripe Mangoes 38
The Kiss 44
Without Within 47
Reflections 48
Dare to be 49
The Farewell 50
Spend the Night 51
Diary of Firewood Deliveryman 54
Leh we go 56
Black Love 57
Crouching Tiger Blush 60
I was alone 63
Tradition or Culture 65
Be No-things 66
She 67
Free your Spoken Words 68

CONTENTS

Follow to Lead……………………………………………………..70
The Book of Annaijh……………………………………………….71
Who lied to us?..74
Your 4th of U-lie…………………………………………………….75
 I am Troy Davis today……………………………………………78
Nah let him fund you……………………………………………...80
Ready or not………………………………………………………..82
Sistah………………………………………………………………..86
 I feel you……………………………………………………………87
 Haiku for Haiti……………………………………………………..90
Love is us……………………………………………………………91
Scent from Heaven………………………………………………...92
The Pros and Cons………………………………………………..94
Dreams and Scars…………………………………………………96
The Wait Game…………………………………………………….97
 Are you game?...99
Drops of Love……………………………………………………...101
Let the Children Play……………………………………………..103
Season of Tears…………………………………………………..105
To be Continued…………………………………………………..109

 The Beginning……………...……………………………..111

Livications

Livicated to those who innerstand and understand that love is the interdependence between all things.

To the mothers who carry life with love that changes their very bodies, tries their mind to breaking but who labor in the night to bring more love to this world.

To the fathers who stand by their sides holding their hands, never letting go of the bond that is love, that will be love.

To love that comes newborn to this world learns and grows to increase the love vibration in this world thru their art.

To change that comes sometimes sooner than later, change that often looks like trouble, but within carries meaning yet to unfold, change that is the storm uprooting trees that no longer needs to be, burying lives that will be missed but not forgotten for this 2 is love.

Pre-word

In searching the many books and writings on the subject of love they all carry virtually the same tone, they regard love in at least four basic forms, (1) unsolicited, unselfish love or love for a perceived divine entity, some call this pure love, (2) love for a sibling or close family member, friend or pet, (3) emotional, or intimate love between sexual partners, (4) maternal love, that which flows from a mother to her child.

These versions all express that love is viewed as an emotion rather than as a faculty such as truth and law, that love was, is and will be whether you and I recognize its existence or not. That love is 'the interdependence between all things' escapes the above categories, so this writer chooses to introduce love from that perspective.

Love is the very fabric from which all of creation is fashioned, the consistency between all things is love, that no-thing exists in and of itself without love, for no- thing exists outside of love. In this regard then the very storm that rips the air asunder, moves trees, elevate the seas, causes life to pass thru the doors of death, this 2 is love.

Turn the pages then as I take you on a journey thru the corridors of love, from the familiar love of intimacy and ecstasy, to the never thought of before love that is the storm, the pain of change, the firm words of warnings and corrections, for this 2 is love.

This 2 is Love

Nothing but love here

I was born with one gray hair
at three
mama took me
to Great-grand and say stay here
children showed me love say come play here
no doors to rooms three to bed
great-grand say come lay here
learnt how to behave here
night was night so beware here
be here when great-grand needed me to be here
grabbed snakes by tails
faced black bull
no fear here
I was born with one gray hair
children listened to any adult who spoke here
considered rude to act like you didn't hear
more rudeness to steups teeth and act like you didn't care
no crimes in the village so no lock to front doors
children could play only after they did chores
no fences to yards what's mines is yours
these are the times in which there was
nothing but love here
to these times I was born with one gray hair
Great-grand would one day tell me what that meant
that I was born with the gift of discernment
to see what is here and what is there
the wisdom to know the difference
I was born with one gray hair

Let Us Love them

Shh!! listen
listen shh!!
can you hear them?
their cries
their sighs
as they finally exhale and proclaim
their disgust at our ignorance
our seemingly semenful lack of substance
can you hear them?

shh!! shh!! listen

they are talking to us
talking about us
pleading with us
to feel them
to lift their burdens
and so heal them
they are tired my brothers
    tired of the burdens they bear
            all by themselves
    tired of the reasons they care
            all by themselves
    tired of the children they rear
            all by themselves
they are tired my brothers
    tired of our ego-tripping
    our slipping
        in and out of their lives as it suits us
            using them as props to boost us
                fools are us

for the abuse we lay at the feet of our queens
our only means of actualizing our purpose
realizing our dreams
                  for we are the stuff dreams are made of
                    the myriad of possibilities
                      that can eternally be
                        that will never be
                if like blind fools we refuse to see
        that they are the wombs
        that shelters our souls
        that feeds our needs
     and gives harvest to our realities
they are the power
that nourishes our will
for what is will void of power
but a newborn without its mother
        they are the mothers
        that tend to our wounds
       at the end of the day
       when the battle is done
                  they are the lovers
                    that love us still
            when we stray from their beds
          and cast our eyes on strange hills
        they are the sisters
        that stand by our sides
       when our heads are hung
        and hands are tied
let us say then to the angry waters
peace be still
so that we may hear their voices
make homes out of houses
and soul mates out of spouses

let us hear their cries
dry their weeping eyes
                let us love them
                          even unto whom they must be
                                    let us protect them
              from the stress of this world
by any means necessary
              I ask you this my brothers
                  if not us
                  then who?
                    listen
                  shh!! shh!!
           can you hear them now?
                  shh!! shh!!
                    listen.

This 2 is love

Naked
I stood upon the banks of the Nile
        giving thanks for awhile
        and for awhile
        time
        seem to stand still
        so still I stood
        like time
        I stand strong

                as gentle breezes brought songs
                      sung long ago
                      to mine ears
                      I hears

years and years of righteous rituals
        echoing on the wind
           as the voices of our sages our messiahs
                calling me from within
                pulling me under
                so I stood still

        so that I may understand
        what say this gentle breeze
        that blows from the East
        and forms
            storm winds of imminent change
                in the West
                then I beheld the dove

      caught in the claws of death
                  I beheld the eagle
                  as a rush of emotion surged thru my being
                          I'm feeling a need to save this dove

                              then before my first eye
                        mountains erupted into the sky
              and the voice of one
      rained down from above

              stand still!! stand still!!

for this too is love
the dove
gives up the ghost
the eagle tightens it claws
then becomes the host
takes to the sky and soars
this fulfills the laws

              stand still!! stand still!!

              for this too is love
          as nature rages from above
              her spoken words echoes in the thunder
                  and under her watchful eyes
                      the lightning strikes
                      not once but twice
                    for this too is love

         see how easily I can write
            of love in the night
             under the bright
                full moon
        the don't come too soon
                  love
                                love that takes its time
                                  the love my body
                                     love my mind
                                            love

                  behold!!

        as black ink is applied to white sheets
      in reverence of that heartbeat for heartbeat
                      love
                                love that crashes the loins
                                 that pries apart two thighs
                               that ties two hearts that joins
   that sweaty, musky, funky love
   from sun-up to sun-down love
                        love that exposes well kept secrets
                        as secretions of life's forces explodes
                        and the balance between life and death
                                                       is tested
                                                            but

                 this too is love
          the fleeting life of the dove
        as the eagle tightens its claws
                 and soars

Love Exposed

I speak of love
not of the uprising mist
formed by rolling stones
not of emotions
not withstanding
                    emotion is but the scent of love exposed
                              yet does not impose
                            though some suppose
                                the world owes
                                        them
                            love comes to shows
                                        them
                  that from the dawn of time love chose
                                        them

for she so loved the world
that she gave her begotten sons and daughters
a gift the world could never repay
                  and if we be that gift
                  then we must lift
                  the word
                  as we lift
                  our minds
                  as we shift
                  in time

forsake the pursuit of Roman dreams
for Rome dreams of black hands in the fields
                  while pale minds uncover stale historical finds
                            then seek to stall the passing of time
                                  while they ponder schemes

                                        dream instead
                dreams dreamt to the beat of drums
dream the drum
and become the beat
I speak of love

Heart beats the Drum

                                        I'm looking for a queen
                                    not seen on every scene
                                                      a rarity
                          like a precious gem to the seeker
                                  she glows with sincerity
                                         see the waves
                      receding daily from the shore
                             she's sometimes un-sure
                            but I'll give her security
                              I'm looking for a queen

I be that shooting star
searching the heavens for its star mate
guided by that magnetic pull of destiny and fate
                                            it's a dark night
                          clouds of feelings and emotions
                              obscure that long sight
                            and sometimes, sometimes
                                  I swear I see her
                              only to be a reflection
                                reflecting within
                              a thousand dewdrops
                                  as night stops
                            and daylight takes flight
                      on the wings of the morning sun
I'm looking for that someone
a woman

                    who knows she's a woman
                    aware of her physicality
                    she lives life thru her spirituality
                         her eyes
                         confident and cool
                                   inflective of her inner-space
                                         her lips taste
                                         like honey dipped truth
                                              succulent
                                         like tree ripened mangoes
                                              she knows
                                              how to call my name
                                         I'm not looking for any games
                                         I'm looking for a queen

                    whose breast is home
                    to a heart of gold
                    comforting in the night
               they bring you joy on a lonely road
                    I snuggle up to them
                         embracing each with a feather light kiss
                              I pay homage to them
                                   for within them
               I hear my name echoed in her heartbeat

                                             the drum-beats
                                             and I'm inside her

                    the drum beats
                    and I'm beside her

the drum beats
and I'm deeply, deeply inside her
she holds me there

                    as my word becomes the bond
               the drumbeats become our heartbeats
                              as her and I become one
                              like the marriage of two
                              in the eclipse of the sun
                         I see my heartbeats in the drum
                                          and I beat
                                              I beat
                                        I beat for her

I'm looking for my queen
have you seen
her?

<u>Stirred not Shaken</u>

These footprints in my mind
are one of a kind
indentations of deep thoughts
made deeper yet
by the thought of you

the thought of you stepping gingerly
yet purposely
with the intention of causing my mind to stir

stirring my mind
with a twist of your hips
the flash of your smile
crossings your lips

stirring my mind
with a soft whisper in my ear
showing me how much you really do care
as my mind stirs

these footprints in my mind
were there from the beginning of our time
when creation of my being
accented an aloneness in my reality
the creator
looked upon the dream-field of my desire
she saw the footprints in my mind
which led to my heart
and there she found you

and from my dreams
formed your essence
into a reality
a reality impressed
with unlimited devotions
undressed emotions
emoting within
the boundless boundaries of
my imagination

a reality which expresses
the infinite thoughts of beauty
these footprints in my mind
are of an idea
whose time has come

After the storm

Sometimes
I move in mysterious ways
night falls
and I dream of mischievous days
shooting balls, toy guns
now serious plays
for sometimes
I move in mysterious ways
Sages say joy comes in the morning
but many mornings have come
many mornings have gone
most have found me
mourning
Pineal stimulations bring flashbacks
fat whips and black back lashes
black bodies raped then draped
in sackcloth and black ashes
Now I rages like the storm in I and I
spitting words of lightening cross the sky
roaring with ancestral thunder
as angels start to cry
teardrops of heavy rain flows
crosswind blows
from whence comes the wrath
they don't know
see now ribbons of rainbows
ring the earth from coast to coast
bringing peace to the masses
when they need it most
for sometimes
I move in mysterious ways

Girl Don't You Know?

My desirable thoughts
are of you
and only you
desiring that you
desire me
to desire you

I wonder 'bout what you're doing
how you're doing it
and why you're doing it

fearing that the pressures of this old world
may take you
then break you
and make you of the mindless
who seek only the limited materials
forsaking the limitless joy of knowing the soul
ignoring the need
as I and I pleads
to be made whole
girl,
don't you know?

don't you understand?
I'm not just another man
but one that can
and will
fulfill
your existence
I mean to enrich your substance

enriched with knowledge of who we are
as we learn to earn each other's respect
and relate
in the likeness of soul mates

enriched with strength for the struggle
as we travel
          on our quest for the truth
          the whole truth
          and nothing but the truth
          lost to our youth
          without roots
          who just wanna loot
          and burn
          without a plan to return
          girl, don't you know?

of the wisdom that is who seeks?
when time stands still for no one
but must be made short
if we are to survive

listen to the birds that sing
always the praise
no matter how hellish the days
their nature will not be deterred
for the word they heard
and so
came to be

listen to the beat of my heart
the beat that gave form to the juju
and beats only for you
come

journey with me to the god-mind
as we seek to avoid the mine fields
planted by the devil- kind
designed to make us blow up
and get large
too large to walk side by side
we pray
and we pray
when time yields to the will of god
and reveals the truth of re-creation
in our fruits

and for the children born to death
                who weeps?
        when fathers and mothers
        refuse to be kings and queens
            but instead
            make separate beds
                as unto the ways of independence
            passing their days like a final sentence
                  when I and I are no more
                    then say no more

                have we become so full of personality
                    our individuality
                that we have forgotten our true identity
from whence comes our life force
                the source of our strength to prevail?

            have we turned each one his own way?
              like a house divided
              will we last the day
            and endure to triumph
              in the last day?

and when the dawn comes
and meets the dusk
will you welcome the setting son
who wills only to rest in your bosom
and nurture my soul under the moon lit sky?

will the ancestors who have risen to stars
give their blessings?

will the words I write
forever enlight
your soul?

will you invite me
to stay
and say
more?
girl
don't you know?

<u>Think supreme</u>

An Afrikan being without an Afrikan mind
is an Afrikan mind trapped
in an Afrikan being
not rooted in the land
as black as his skin
taught to refute the hand
that guided him

to rebel against the two
that thought of him
welcomed him
to a world that needed him
thoughts of him conceived
before his baba seeded him
in the womb of the nurturer who read to him
and feeded him

I could have said fed
but instead
I deliberated then deliberately
broke their rules
like breaking chains of a language
that binds our minds
our language is hidden in our minds
but not lost to our minds
for language is a product of thought
and thoughts are electro-magnetic impulses
pulsating from the mind that thought of us

That mind is supreme
and so is the Afrikan
to think Afrikan is to think supreme
                                                  but not superior
                                                  then we will remember
                      that our language is not inferior
from coast to coast
to the heart and the interior
remembrance will take us beyond Kiswahili and Twi
                                      back to the hieroglyphics
                                      and supreme mathematics
to the language of the universe
back to the mother tongue

When thoughts were relayed without the tongue
scriptures scripted
but no pages flipped
no rages between bloods and crypts
plantation politics then flipped the script
but now it's time to trip that Afrikan switch
ignite that Afrikan light
come
let us think supreme again
let us think Afrikan again

FORGIVENESS IS A PROCESS

Many are writing off wrongs against them under the misconception that they are forgiving their debtors this is a dangerous practice to the mind for there can be no forgiveness without repentance.

The act of writing off the wrong is selfish, it allows one to move the debt off their active balance sheets into an inactive file, once written off you stop actively pursuing(thinking about) this debt, similar to the criminal system's cold case files, that does not mean the debt(wrongful act against you) does not still exist. In most cases when a debt is written off the one who owes is not aware that the debt has been written off, while the one who is owed now has peace of mind because they are no longer thinking about this debt, the one who owes still bears the burden of what they owe and may in time come forward and settle the debt, the one who is owed may then bring the debt out of the inactive file and forgive it.

When the debt is forgiven, there is a dance between the wronged and the perpetrator that involves the perpetrator (1) acknowledging that they offended (2) vowing not to repeat the offense (3) asking for forgiveness of the offense. This is the unique opportunity for the wronged to not move the offense to an inactive file but completely wipe it out. Forgiveness is a process that actively involves both the perpetrator and the wronged.

Sister, forgive me

Once upon a time
there was love between us
mutual respect
mutual trust
we were truly family
familiar with each other's wants
and needs-to-be
        you were then the apple of mine eye
          then for you I would gladly die
            but enter now the element of the distrust
              that two-tongue serpent amongst us
              some would have you bear the blame
              accuse you of falling victim to the game
              but from this day let the truth be known
                it is I who abdicated the throne
for though you unwittingly invited the evil in
it is my ignorance that completed the sin
for I lost it that night
blinded by the atomic light
of that first big fight
abusing you concerned me the least
            as I succumbed to the rage
             here comes the beast
              in that very hour
         we felt the warmth of the sun
             departing the east

                    for in abusing you
              I placed my concerns above yours
          and like the night shutting down the sun
                  I closed the family doors
                  dividing the atomic energy
                   into what's mine is mine
                    what's yours is yours
                              shifting our consciousness
                                    to the lessor individual
                                       debasing our identity
                                      to that of the animal
                              struggling daily just for survival
              but gods-to-be do more than just survive
                  for we can and must revive
                  those who sleep like the dead
                  and feed to the hungry souls
                     spoken words like bread
               then I sold you to the highest bidder
come now bigger the nigger be bitter
as poisoned waters flow the river Nile
and for a while
I hardly realized
I had sold the most desirable part of me
                        but now this madness consumes me
                             and confuses me to no end
                                          forgive me
                                for I know not what I do
                                       for without you
                           I am but a one winged eagle
                                    caught in a storm

and the creator in her own wise-dome
none higher
has delivered us into the land of strangers
into the fire
for there we were to seek each other
like level to the water
but like a heavy stone we sank
breaking ranks
we ate swine and drank
I renamed you shorty
as I rallied to the forty
not the promised acres and the mules
but the colt and the malt
that turned our bloods to blues
and kings to the fools
for I sold your back that day
by looking the other way
in exchange for their definition of success
you then his slave girl by day
by night his mistress
I sold you crack to blow your mind
to remind you of your emptiness
your life's distress
I sold your back uptown and downtown
on every street corner in this damnation
I confined you to those "strip your soul" bars
where fools the niggas parade their fancy cars
disguising their ill-begotten stripes and scars
and while you foolishly trade the most precious prize
for a handful of Abes
and his gang-full of red dead blue eyes

                I ignore your pain
            as you spread your thighs
          exposing the core of the apple
         I've been programmed to despise
        and so we alienate each other
              with our untrustworthy insecure behavior
                    me driving miss daisy
                      you like crazy
            into the arms of corporate America
                  that twisted character
         where you mate with the beasts
           the carrier of dis-eases
         forming cancerous family ties
       bonding with that two-tongued serpent
           his games, his tricks, his lies
me now to his armed forces
where soul sources
are stripped, searched and destroyed
come now unemployed
some say vets
the me-nots
they'd like to forget
              and while their counterfeit degrees
                some so steadfastly pursue
           our deliverance comes in realizing
              the love that binds me to you
                   so come

let us be then unto each
as brother and sister
unto children
as mother and father
kings and queens unto our culture
once upon a time we were family
I know that I have not been all that I can be
but sister
can you please forgive me?

DJANGO UNCHAINED (Critiqued)

Hollywood's intent was never to entertain the African but to use the African as entertainment for the European.

Hollywood is a media controlled by those who control the banks and move heads of States around like chess pieces, their supreme intent is to maintain a specific world order that has the African playing the role of supporting cast to the European star.

To you it's only a movie and movies are not real, so why are you still afraid of the dark? How did you feel months even years after you saw the Omen and other such movies that are not real? How many young men felt like martial arts experts after seeing Bruce Lee in enter the dragon? How many actually went on to pursue their degrees and became experts because of how that movie that is not real made them feel?

What the mind perceives as real is real to the mind, if it's real to the mind the mind will direct the brain to respond accordingly.

Tarantino mixed an emotional cocktail using laughter and pain and served this to an unwitting audience. Both the European (Yurugu) and the African laughed openly at the folly of the KKK and other such scenes with the African's pain of the MAAFA as the backdrop to these hilarious moments, but the mind only works in absolutes, so laughing at those scenes which were conjured up back dropped against those painful scenes that actually occurred was also laughing at those painful scenes which equated to laughing at our ancestors pain of the MAAFA. Yurugu is also laughing at the conjured up scene right next to the African and in the middle of that laughter without warning the most horrific scenes of actual torture of the African was presented, but the laughter was not immediately curtailed so both Yurugu and the African were caught openly laughing while the flesh was being torn from the backs of the African.

The entire 2+ hours of this movie was engineered for the scene of less than 5 minutes, that's how programming works. This is the scene in which the skull was revealed (SKULL AND BONES) and Leonardo who plays Candy (sweets to appeal to the childlike mind which is present during laughter and pain) spills his blood while delving into their supreme lie that the African is inherently inferior and submissive to the European, he does this while cracking the skull open and appearing to display scientific proof which was the only scene that was not refuted by the know it all Yurugu that Django was indebted to.

Where there is no refutation the mind in its now pliable state will accept this suggestion that was not dwelt on but simply dropped in the mind like a seed in the ground as fact. The African children watching this movie are the real victims.

WAKE UP AFRICAN YOU ARE DREAMING!!

Movie criticism by Rudwaan

Tis their season

Where young trees shaped like pyramids
are killed then decorated
then dead trees planted in living rooms
like dead seeds planted in living wombs
they soon go toxic
we wonder then why the children are born sick
tis their season
we fall hard for their lies and tricks
longing for a piece of their rotten American pie
our elders moan
while the young die quick
Tis their season

Young trees are hewn from their roots
grown to bear no fruits
harvested for yurugu's pleasure
treasure for a day
then they meet the fire
Tis their season we are programmed to admire
bedazzled by the decapitated heads of African orphans
hanging ornamentally from dead trees
we see lights but refuse to see the light
then wonder why our land is blight
as vultures like santa drop from flight
to feed on the souls of our able and might
Tis their season

where bells are jingled from coast to coast
and hell is mingled with heavenly hosts
          as satan some say santa tightens the reins
         around the necks of those we hold deer
baba working two jobs can't afford the partridge or the tree
              so he buys the pear
      here comes satan down the chimney
        to replace baba in the night
      we wonder why our village ain't right
      tis their season
where death walks the earth
red with the blood of slain African children
whose flesh adorn dead trees shaped like pyramids
as eyeballs dangle from dead limbs twinkle like lights
and choirs go from house to house to sing oh holy nights
      our ancestors moan
   as African heads are mounted
atop dead trees like pyramid capstones
     tis their season

                   but truth be told
                    tis the season
            when nature hibernates
       when gods release earth-bound lust
              and bury unborn hates
       tis the season
for the sun to die in the west
to fall into deep slumber
and dream new sons awake
      tis the season
where life rests beneath frozen lakes
      tis the season
to throw off yearlong burdens and deeply bury
but to the vampires and werewolves it's twilight
      so
tis their season to be merry

while we work our fingers to the bones
to keep up with Smith and Jones
can you hear their santa
with his reins around the necks of our dear ones
calling us hoe, hoe, hoes?
Tis their season.

Two Dreams Dancing

I am the rising Son
the one on whom the sun rises
and sets the sons of mothers in motion
like waves of devotion
rising from her mighty ocean
bringing our dreams to shore
surely I've seen visions
sunrays dancing with moonbeams
like two dreams dancing
on a bed of sweet creams
I've seen the Yin
walking hand in hand with the yang
reminiscing on days of that ole love thang
and bang
was the sound heard
when griots gripped the mic
with songs and spoken words
dormant thoughts hit the airwaves
and exploded
six million ways to live one life
were deeply planted
traveling the inner recesses of her chocolate milky way
storms of convulsive passions erupting
causing aimless travelers to go astray
and I am the rising son
the one who must enter the sacred womb
to be born
so I stay steadfast to the course
seeing mine own fall to the wayside
I am counting the loss

searching for a planet green with life
not yet explored
seeing sights
hearing sounds
too beautiful to be ignored
                with open arms she welcomes me home
                                    and now
                            I am the setting Sun
                    yielding the sky to her rising moon
full and pregnant with the promise
that the son will rise again

Be here

A lot of dreams died here
schemes tried here
friends lied here

Dreams can be re-born here
schemes weaved can come undone here
and friends can be friends when the war is done here

But who dares to fear here?
they who have ears let them hear here
come come! here here!

Standing ovation for she who bears here
gives birth to those with nappy hair
happy to be here

Behold a dream is re-born here
schemes weaved failed to undo here
be in the moment
be here

The wanting

I wanted to think of you today
just because I wanted to
it happened just as I wanted it to
I don't regret wanting to
you would not want me to
I want you too
I want you to
want me
too

Ripe Mangoes

I spoke to my cousin the other day
I asked of him
how things were
and he replied
Mangoes are in season this time of year
and they are ripe
their scent permeates the atmosphere
causing the neighborhood children
to trespass without care
in search of that which produces
such a magnetic aroma
arousing pre-pube passions
not yet learned of

My cousin chose to relate this to me
for on the island of Tobago
where I grew
and he still grows
the family property is home to a mangrove
which in turn is home to several mango trees
and it is in this mangrove
where we spent our waking day
when school was out
this is where we played our games
and bonded
as cousins, as brothers, as young warriors

Seeking to stir my imagination further
I asked my cousin to describe
in as much detail as possible
the mangoes on the tree
he again replied
well…
                      They're hanging ever so precariously
                          from stems
                                    gingerly attached to limbs
                                      that defiantly protrude
                                          from deeply rooted
                                            robustly standing
                                                tree trunks
                they hunger for the earth below
                        and I know
                the earth wants them too
                        for sure
                the earthworms do
                      we laughed

                                    this prosaic piece however
                              is not entirely about mangoes
                    nor is it about the grove in which they grow
not about the neighborhood children
who trespass there
nor my overly indulging cousin
whom I speak to about twice a year
I simply recalled this conversation
when she came into view

She walked perfectly
my heart skipped the beats
her steps refused to
her gait
straight
and proud
she seemed to be carried along
on a thin strip of cloud
making the motion of walking
simply for posterity
her feet
hardly seemed to touch the ground
her steps
made no sound
to not see her
one would not know
she was there
her hair
jet black half-dreaded
dropped wavily down her back
like water falling from the cliffs of Niagara
they did not fall to the earth however
for they were not too soon braced
as I uttered
there but for the grace

She wore black
she was black
with just a slight hint of macadamia
in her skin tone
she walked alone

Should I approach?
my mind reasoned
but I quickly calculated
some things are best left as they are
this beauty I would admire from afar

        As she slowly walked out of view
           my eyes willingly settled
on that which prevented the long locks of hair
            from reaching the earth
              I often wondered
where do full moons go
when their course is done?
it appeared to me
she took her responsibility
quite seriously
for she carried the full moon
quite carefully
in her back pockets
            what puzzled me however
        was the fact that she had no back-pockets
                but rather

        Her statue was draped delicately
         in a simple one-piece mid-thigh
                black dress

                                    now my bepuzzlement grew
                                            was she the moon
                                                 full and ripe
                                     like the season of mangoes
                                    sumptuously balanced
                                    on what I deduced to be
two of the seven wonders of creation
perfect pillars of flesh
hued from the finest mahogany
set aside since the dawn of time
              awaiting her physical manifestation
              wind blasted into sandpaper quality
                    by the very breath of yah?
                            whew!!
                    she took my breath away

                                Suddenly, I smelled mangoes
                                             they were ripe
                                           and I grew hungry

               I did not see her eyes
              and deep down inside
                  I'm glad I did not
the eyes being the window to the soul
and all that
what if her soul was not all that
then I would be left with but
a lustful hunger
no longer
the righteous respect
and deep admiration
for this beauty of creation
that I was blessed to bear witness to
she was gone

and I went to the Patti Hut Café
and ordered a Tobago bash
made of papaya, coconut and mangoes
yep
ripe mangoes

<u>The Kiss</u>

I be going down
like the sun setting down
in all his glory
and I hear sounds
like waterfalls underground
echoes of our story
                      fools lose their way
               thru valleys of cool breezes
but gods find paths
to the lake that pleases
where heads bow in reverence
between wholly creases
       imagery of light being one with darkness
             draws me closer
              and I kiss
                      I kiss the lips that seal
                        your private places
                   traces of wet tongue strokes
                            provokes
                 musky emissions to emote
     hands slide slowly over oil slick flesh
     fresh flowers fill the air like sweet funk
                I dunk
over and over into your valley of life
where dry bones are made wet
                jet black
         strands of your welcome mat glistens
            silence listens
              at your door
as pinkish lips swollen with desire
            pleads for moor

                              metaphors unfold
                              my tongue swirls
                              you dream worlds
                              into existence
                        increasing my persistence
                  I go deeper
nearer my god-head to thee
bearer of the seventh key
that unlocks the door
to your inner chamber
I knocks three times
then enter
there I saw visions
I saw the yin
walking hand in hand with the yang
                  reminiscing
                        on the days of that ole love thang
                              I saw dreams
                        dreaming of beats to come
                  as hums become
incoherent groans in motion
I be the sun going down in his glory
as talently my tongue titillates
            the intricate cracks and crevices of your reality
                              and I be wondering
                        if my best be good enough
                  failing this test could hurt so much
            in so much as
            the more I reveal
            the more you feel
            the more I must reveal
            I say
            the more we must heal
                  so come

                    dance this day in my dreams
              where sunrays be dancing with moon beams
            where yin be one with yang on a bed of sweet creams
your cream be rising to the top now
screams to stop now
suppressed
expressed
undressed
                I smell the aroma of funk and poetry
                    I feel you wooing me
                    should I go crazy
                         as your resistance goes lazy
                              drop to my knees
                              as my eyes goes hazy?
                              here comes the night
                              like a cup that runneth
                                   the Nile cometh
                              over and over her banks
                              her divine way of giving thanks
the overflow drenches your nappy bushes
I sips then pushes
as mountains like hips cry out
Byrd takes flight
as miles ahead
the Coltrane shouts
peace follows the wholly storm
two souls enter
one is born
now the final sunrays
dresses the waning horizon for bedtime
                                   wet tongue strokes
                              caresses your inner sanctum
                         one last time
              and angels bowed their heads in bliss
                         to the kiss

__Without Within__

            Existence is broken without
                      within
no love is spoken
love is but a token
      a mere word spoken without
                  within
love beckons us
    to mend the broken pieces without
              without within
within will be
but without will not see
                  within
existence is broken
words spoken
are but empty vessels
        without the love from within
existence is broken
           we can't see within
           without within

Reflections

The sky is the mind of the earth

the clouds are her wombs

black and pregnant with the waters of life

she blinks an eye and the lightning flashes

probing the very crevices of your mind

hoping to find

that you are ready to be born

again

as we

ase

Dare to be

It's the fear that we fear
that makes us hear what we hear
wear what we wear
bear what we bear
some say vote or die
I say do not dare
give your life for that lie
devote instead
to the laws of the Most High
and dare to be
on purpose

The farewell

I remember when
you didn't have two nickels to rub together
took you in
gave your head cover
you were vulnerable
could have made you my lover
but I gave you room to breathe
to get yourself together

Nothing in return did I expect
just was not prepared for the dis-respect
so I showed you the door
told you
not to come round no more
you see

I just wanted to be good to you
you said you've been thru so much
just wanted to be the man who stood with you
but the closer I got to you
the clearer I saw you
the stories you told were loosely molded
as lies you held slowly unfolded

I simply couldn't be part of it
certainly not a starring role in it
I hope you find your soul in it
now we've reached the end of it
so farewell
be well
be

Spend The Night

Come,
spend the night
under this canopy of twinkling stars
where night-wears reveal
what in daytime we conceal
reactions
from those who react like nucleic fusion
actors
they act like stars
while poets?
poets spill the beans on mass confusion
feeding the masses
with soul food solutions
spend the night
        spend the night like the sun
          who spends and spins
         all his time around her
            adoring her
         her natural formations
          erect manifestations
           that rise and fall
    to the heat of his perfect luminations
           unlocking doors
        with mental combinations
          spend the night
          and see the sun

see the sun as he sets
and glows him down to sleep
rays old like griots
his soul to keep
magnificent radiance reflecting
reflections of ecstasy and pain
like that painting in time
we be born again
then we be torn again
he sheds a tear
at her serpentine hillsides
her bulbous endowments
earth tone earthly enshrubments
her mountains
peaked with chocolate-like scorched earth
turned black by one too many convulsions
eruptions of the most high
why?
spend the night
and listen

listen as nature's night songs
echoes her final call
leaves fall
to knees of the very trees
who bore them
I saw them
I saw the son
becoming one
with her

his final rays of hope
finds their way to her valleys
as Lazarus rises from dark alleys
and comes forth
looks to the north
where she splits herself in two
who hears the night
when she comes for you?
for she be
mother to the sun
lover to the one
so come
spend the night
and listen

Diary of a firewood delivery man

It was a cold night
the moon seemed frozen
against the black sky
Prince crooned from the stereo
'when doves cry'
a soft glow lit the room
slender shadow slid slowly
as if from the womb
before I saw her
    I smelled the delicate fragrance of her perfume
framed in a red teddy
she was ready
to bloom
she gestured me slowly
towards her fireplace
it was a cold night
prayers answered
someone to hold tight
tonight fires would ignite
    wood set ablaze
        firewood set gently in place
        but not with haste
        she wore lace
        removed yes I did
        to reveal her enclosed space
        more wood she moaned
        as fire kissed her face
        fire hissed loudly
        from her fireplace

wood snapped and crackled
as I urgently poked it
fire blazed and licked
at her inner walls
two balls
ice-cubes melted
            against the rising heat
                      rising to my feet
                      beads of sweat falling
                      cell phone calling
                      it was a cold night
                      I was on call tonight
              I hoped against odds
            no one else would call tonight
            but this caller I knew all too well
       her fire-place was always in need of wood
                    and she paid all too well
                      she lived across town
                      and traffic was light
              be there in thirty I said
              I know it's a cold night
          the soft voice brought me back
              to my present moment
              I know my time is up
                and you have to go
but before you walk out that door
this wood would need to be poked
a little bit more

Leh We Go

When the outcome is tied to our ego
the outcome will always be so so
let go of the ego
and leh we go
higher

Black Love

You
are the wetness
of the summer rain
I fall for
in my hour of pain
yours is the name
I call for
and when you need
a helping hand girl
you are the one
I give my all for

you say you're looking
for a man that's true
who'll love
honor
respect
and be good to you

hold you in the night
when you need it most
be there in the morning
with herbal teas and toast

make you giggle like a little girl
as he teases your toes
gentle kisses, soft pecks
as he removes your clothes

lay you on your back
break out the body cream
take his time from the back
as you purr and scream

                    tug on your locks
                    as he rocks your world
                    then whispers in your ear
                    keep your head up girl

for you
are the wetness
of the summer rain
I fall for
in my hour of pain
yours is the name
I call for
and when you need
a helping hand girl
you are the one
I give my all for
                    now I'll be lying
                    if I say I didn't feel you
                    but more than an itch to scratch
                    girl I wanna be real with you
                    if you hungry and I ain't gots
                    the world I'll steal for you
                    and when it's time for prayer
                    I swear
                    I'll kneel with you
                              for your value is invaluable
                              no man can put a price to you
                              seeing you vulnerable like this
                              I can't help but be nice to you
                    so indulge me if you will
                    let me kick this advice to you
                    seek your divinity like Mary
                    and let me be Christ to you
                    I'll give my life for you

for my life's pledge is to
love
honor
and protect you
respect you
the morning after the night
I stepped to you
the night heaven rained down black love
and I wept with you
for you
are the wetness
of the summer rain
I fall for
in my hour of pain
yours is the name
I call for
and when you need
a helping hand girl
you are the one
you are the one
you are the one
I give my all for

Crouching Tiger Blush

Bloodlines bulged
with life thru thickened veins
sweet names dripped
like drops of springtime rains
names like "Precious", like "Queen"
baby doll adorned her Nubian frame
she feigned shyness
I whispered "your highness"
as slowly towards her canopy throne I came
if only like a warrior
fresh and strong from battle
to she?
I be the genie
just released from the bottle
slowly I move pass lamp
propped on bedside table
damp swelts form puddles
just inside her navel
reverently I approached
bearing gifts
ready, willing and able
'my king' she uttered
words barely escaped
the prizm of breath
as I touched her gently
just beyond
where secrets are kept

                    shivered she did
                      as black lace
                         I slid
                      from its place
                   back where love did bid
                        me near
                       there I saw
               the mound where gold was hid
               and swear the voices of angels
                       I did hear
'kiss me there' she breathed
with bedroom eyes she plead
as lips I licked as if to say
my darling but indeed
                        now nose knows now
                 the sweet scent of her 'I'm ready' smells
                                           blood rush
                                  as crouching tiger blush
                                   behind bush in crotch
                                     where five dwells
                  inspired by whiffs and blasts
                      of her aromatic spells
                      anxiously I dispense
                   with the last of my outward shells
"down south" she muttered
her body shivered and shuttered
like a soothing Caribbean breeze
                         I blew
                        I teased
                        she flew

I nibbled slowly at the valley
then nuzzled her
totally I commit my lips
air-brush left nip
being ever so careful
not to puzzle her
      she groans now
      me moans now
   erotic zones be prone to set the tone now
        as lone-eye peeps thru pee-hole
          sees her tee-hole
         she seizes me-pole
        and guides me home now
     home at last
     home at last
    thank god almighty
    we home at last

I Was Alone

Before I thought of you
there was only me
and I was alone
no things existed
not even the unknown
and in my aloneness
I knew not loneliness
for no thoughts prevailed
I was conscious
only of mine own consciousness
I was none
not even one
no not one
      no measure could be made unto me
        none other to relate with
      to debate with
   to love, honor and vibrate with
      then you stirred in me
         and in that moment let there be one
          resonated from the nothingness
           the thought of you
          became a manifestation of me
           and I was one with you
            born of nothings
        you are the embodiment of all things
       you are the oneness
      perfection
   a reflection of my none-ness
     thru you shall all things be
       so come

                    let us make man in our own image
                    male and female create us them
                       let his mind be sound
                        his character strong
make her
the bearer of truth
thru and thru
make her
as unto the most desirable part of you
                            let him carry the seeds of possibilities
                              possess in her the power of actualities
                            let him dream
                                she will make his dreams realities
                         let him be as unto the key
                            she is the door
                            thru which new suns
                            and full moons are born
                         the children were the first day

Afrikan tradition or Afrikan culture

Some traditions are deviations due to disagreeable minds much like the various forms of so-called re-ligions we find ourselves in today.

Yet other traditions may have developed to meet requirements of the times and when times no longer require then those traditions ought to be retired. Traditions may come and go as needed, but the culture remains.

No cell in the body is greater than another, each cell has its purpose and its purpose is just as important and worthwhile as every other cell.

Traditional practices that develop a hierarchical system
wherein certain members of the community
are viewed as less worthwhile than others
should be viewed with much skepticism
To be Afrikan
is to be
divine.

__Be No-things__

Like the child in us
we just wanna own things
want our own things
each one wishing
to be a known thing
                    unknowing to each
                we be umbilically connected
                    to unknown things
but now we be grown beings
we should knowingly put aside all-things
and go inside no-things
for therein
all-things become known things
be nothings
and all-things will be possible
some things will unlock like parables
and from a distance look like trouble
but fear not
    for all things unto no-things must be humble
        even the rumble in the heavens
            bow to the spoken word
                for from the consciousness of no-things
                          came the word
                    and so all things came to be
            yet some dis-own the word
            in praise of things to own
some have grown into the word
and be with her in the beginning
own nothing
and no-thing owns you

She

How can a man fly
if the wind won't blow for him
if the earth won't grow for him
what would he eat
If the rains won't fall for him
what would he drink
if the sun won't die for him
when will he rest
If the trees won't sway for him
when his mother ceases to pray for him
who would stand with him
When the days grow short for him
who would be there to comfort him
to show love to him?
How can a man fly
if he constantly abuses
his power supply
who would he be
if it weren't for she?

Free your Spoken Words

Time be now to express divine gifts
to impress on the mind
we shift to lift
see lost boys like ships drift
closer to mothers on seashores
fathers stand up and claim yours
as angels punch the clock I saw
                          men like eagles take to the sky and soar
                          microphones checked from door to door
                                        moods change
                                    colors re-arrange
                            dark souls dance in the light
                    as grounded consciousness takes flight
free you spoken words of malice and fore-thought
where after thoughts become thoughts of guilt
like that house that jack built
build your thoughts
with thoughts
that gods thought
                thoughts that calm the raging seas
                      that calls to the wind
                and cause to be or not to be
        thoughts that tap the dead-zone of the brain
           as words of power calls forth purple rain
                      worlds of impossibilities
                            become possible
            homicides no longer justifiable
           probable causes no longer probable
                parables soar like eagles
           and parallel park next to legals

            poets need no permit
             to drop the science
          poets need no contracts
              to see the signs
     to those begotten sons and daughters
            who walks on water
   crossing bridges of ancestral martyrs
let each one teach one
to remember now
producing schematics of images
that be
energies like we
        we be the dreamers of this universe
          for we be the gods that bless
          and we be the gods that curse
so shift your words of power
lift up your words this hour
for ours is the kingdom
and the glory
forever and ever
amen

Follow to Lead

A leader is not one that has followers
but one who has achieved the seat of leadership
in his/her being
and is now in a position to encourage others
to do the same.

Those so called leaders
who see themselves as shepherds
must likewise see their audience as sheep,
reducing a divine being to the mental reality of a sheep
(one who will eternally follow)
is the work of a predatory leader.

A predatory leader is
one who thrives on co-dependent relationships
wherein they are leaders for life
and their audiences are followers for life,
always seeking but never quite finding.
To be Afrikan is to be A Free Being
pursuing the seat of leadership within
in order to realize his/her Supreme Being
while walking the earth.
Follow your leader within and become.

The Book of Annaijh
Chapter Nine: Strong Medicine

The preacher said
God reached down and took her
at the age of nine
God chose to close life's book on her
God being God
could have simply withheld life's breath from her
but instead to her
God sent to her
a bullet to the precious and tender head of her
                                           But I disagree
                               with this preacher's account of her
                              for God didn't issue a recall that day
                                                 on her
                                    didn't wake with her
                         and decided to expand the heavenly hosts
                                            with her
                             no holy ghosts and sons
                             longed for the company of her
                                   no mistah preacher
                     I disagree with your account of her
I count her years on ten fingers
and am left with one remainder
a reminder
that we the village
failed to raise the child in her
now we raise voices sing songs
praise the child in her
light candles hold vigils
and recall the oh so few days of her
caravans of cars and buses
lead to graveyards where we bury her

but let's not bury our heads in the sand with her
less we fully account for why
this happened to her
we'll be caravanning again and again
to bury another and another
Annaijh died
because we the village
failed to raise the child in her
We failed her with our silence
while evil hustled and grinded around her
we chose to honor codes
that tells us not to tell
that evil swells and dwells
around her
raising hell
around her

We failed her with our ignorance
as we ignored the violent weeds
growing around her
threatening the life of this
yet to bloom flower
we valued them weeds
more than we did her
them weeds paying folks rent
with paper derived
from exploiting children just like her
the village failed
to raise the child in her

We failed her with our impotence
rims and dogs carry more importance
them rims and things get our undivided attention
as they spin and shine with brilliance
we'll never see her full brilliance
them dogs are well-groomed
well-fed
well cared for
                    single mothers struggle with these children
                        while struggling to stay on welfare
                    we spend more time in the company of dogs
                                walking them
                                talking to them
                              playing with them
                  our children are left to play on their own
                 where are the fathers to watch over them
                            watch-out for them
                        to praise them as they play
                            to encourage them
                like we "that's a good boy" them dogs
We the village failed to raise her
to raise her life's worth
above dogs and rims
now Annaijh is dead
with a bullet to the head
by one of those dogs
no mistah preacher
God didn't take her
we the village sent her
                    it takes a village to raise but one Annaijh
                              let's not fail the others
                              let us move the village

to the memory of Annaijh Rolax

Who lied to us?

Our children have come now to make us hard
to make us fearless
though they may be sometimes careless
we should not care less
instead be care full
less we forget
to ignore once
is ignorance

we romance the struggle
we love the struggle
we struggle for the struggle
don't take away our struggle
we will die without our struggle
who lied to us?
Our children have come to make us hard

YOUR 4TH OF U-LIE

Your 4th of July **is a lie**
It's a lie
that you discovered this land
or any land for that matter
this land was not lost
we were here
and so were the indigenous peoples you called Indians.
It is you who lost your way
tripped over Plymouth Rock
and landed in our back-yard.
U-LIE!

It's a lie
that you developed this land
the Moors were already here
with irrigation systems
crop rotations
communication systems
education systems
and many other systems
that comprise self-governance
we lived in synergistic harmony with the land
you on the other hand
were pillaging each other
raping each other
sacking each other

lacking a competent sewage system
you suffered and died of the many diseases
developed from your undiscarded feces
so as far as development goes
it is to be said to your credit
you developed diseases
U-LIE!

it's a lie
that you brought civilization to an uncivilized people
it is we who found you dying of starvation and diseases
we nurtured you
fed you
healed you
taught you how to grow crops
how to hunt
how to build shelters
how to wipe your very asses
and like the parasites you are
you suppressed your hosts
compromised our immune system
with your highly mutated diseases
which includes
your school to prison pipeline mis-education system
your just-us illegal system
your greedy capitalistic banking and usury system
these are your true weapons of mass destruction
you raped and killed women
children
castrated and scalped men
relegated your hosts to plantations and reservations
you civilized whom?
U-LIE!

You then set about to under-develop the land
by plastering her skin with poisonous asphalts
you killed the great lakes
your oil-spills and hunt for the thrill of the kill
compromise the Eco-system from pole to pole
you deforested rain-forests which serve as herbal centers
only to replace them with drug-stores
political whores
as banking cartels wage world wars
U-LIE!

It's a lie
that in 1776 you gained independence from your parents
the Stolen Crown
for there is no such thing as independence
for not even a parasite can survive and thrive
independent of its host
Europe could not and would not exist today
without the human and material resources they stole
and is still stealing from Afrika
even a newborn baby knows
that all things are inter-dependent
and no-thing exists by itself
from itself
unto itself
because of itself
So the very foundation of your 4th of July
which is **your independence day is a lie**
therefore we endorse and support this day
as your 4th of **U-LIE!**
U-LIE!
U-LIE!

I AM TROY DAVIS TODAY

Yesterday I was Sean Bell, Amadou Diallo
so many others how far will this go
how long will we gag on this diet
from he who oppresses
hold the presses
this just in

another African killed by injustice
I am Troy Davis
Today

no doubt about it their system is unjust
but that's not the only thing killing us
black people wake up we're killing us
the shame and pain of the MAAFA is still in us
black boys filled with self-hate be stealing us
I am Troy Davis today

but who will stand now and say I am Tayshana Murphy
she was only 15 they say it was mistaken identity
he was black, she was black
where's the mistake in that

stop lying to yourselves Black people
if we really be Troy Davis the frequency would ripple
black hoods would be the safest place for Black People
but instead we're hunted by the hunter and the hunted
triple deep dead bolts got imaginations stunted
black blocks framed with bars on windows
pipeline to cell blocks where bars lock
and black casts no shadows
I am Troy Davis
today

tomorrow
I'll go back to being the demon that haunts the hood
that crack dealer dealing death to black wombs
black women stripping souls on poles
paying rent in private rooms
I'll be that black pimp for whom
that little black girl walks in the moon
the gang-banger gang banging black boys
into black men too soon

but until the needle hits the vein
I'll respond and say
I am Troy Davis
Today

Nah let him fund you

Who funds you runs you
fail dem den dem bun you
come down dodo dem ground you
dem can't own you six under dem down you
like monkey see den monkey do dem clown you

give dem inch dem tek boat foot from you
reach in mout tek teet tongue from you

but how come you trust
the same who tar feathered and hung you
same who stole name, culture, land from you
raise right hand and swear in court he never wrong you
rape your women
beat your children
kill your elders in front of you?

what else must he do to prove him no man to you?
him beast to you
the greatest of him less than the least of you
inside of you is the greatest gift to you
love of life will lift the very down-trod of you
up you mighty people remember
together you be Gods to you
ancient songs and verses were written in regards to you

listen closely African and hear your roots speak to you
his-story folds as yours unfolds
signs tell
bell tolls
the truth speaks for you
reparations is the key
that unlocks the bars of time around you
hear the poets rhyme
free your African mind inside you
you existed
even before the elements of time formed around you
is lies him tell when him say hymn found you
take care of each other African
and one last ting
nah let him fund you

<u>Ready or Not</u>

I remember when
in the days of children
we would play then
and say then
you go hide
and I'll come seek you
                    and as children do
                    we did
                    I would count to ten
                    while you hid
                    and we would play our games
                    all day long
                    ignoring time
                    till the setting sun
                    begging him to stay with us
                    to play with us
                    one more hour
          as grandma's yell echoed thru the woods
                    time for suppa
and we knew what time it was
without a timepiece
we knew the hour was at hand
for we were the children of the play
the children of the times
and we knew the signs
the sun

slowly closing his eyes
taking with him the daylight
water frogs croaking incessantly
welcoming the night
cricket chirping
bats taking flight
grandma's yell permeating like a microphone
calling all the young playahs home
and it must have been a naturally known fact
for all of nature seemed to join in the act
as creatures great and small
echoed their own final call
and we knew what time it was
                                time now for the last play of the day
                            this play we would dream of as we slept
                                this play set our nerves on edge
                                        for on this play
                              we had no time to do it again
                                    no time to screw up
for now the sun was like a red ball of fire
falling from the sky
and grandma's final call would find I and I
and so you went to hiding
as I started counting
we knew what time it was
for it was on
the final countdown had begun

and like Tehuti's horn
sounding thru the heavens
my yell of ten trumpeted thru the trees
and like all of a sudden
all
was perfectly still
as if in anticipation of some rapture
this was the final chapter
this is the moment we played our whole day for
as more and more
the sun died in the west
only to rise in the east
where Kilimanjaro rests
and I heard the sound of the evening wind
rustling thru the trees
as I lifted my voice
and screamed against the impending night
ready or not
here I come
and I found you
where I knew you would be
now the game was over
and so was the day
for the tone of grandma's yell
found us and told us
she won't be yelling no more
and we knew what time it was
it was time now to go home
but this prosaic feature
is not about children's games
for we have no time to play them
not about nature's night creatures
nor grandmother's yelling names

                    this trek down memory lane
                  is a wake-up call under cover
                            an alarm sounding
                  calling us from under the covers
                         a warning of sorts
                       that it's time to get up
for the signs of the times
are here, there and everywhere
and just like the games that children play
this night will soon end
and the sun will come back again
sending his brilliant rays of hope
his brilliant strategy for a new day
                              to seek us
                              to find us
                             to lift us up
                       will we be found ready?
                              or not?

Sistah

I'm looking for a strong sistah to roll with
grief comes knocking to console with
wealth start flowing to control with
cold winter nights to hold with
bad hand dealt to fold with
recreate and mold with
to be involved with
be in love with
resolve with
evolve with
see with
be with
within

I feel you

You say to the descendant of the Spaniard
the Portuguese
the same who man the slave ship Jesus
kidnapped and brought your ancestors
to these shores and others
who now look at you like you a piece a meat
hanging from a hook
yuh tellim im good man
empower im with yuh eye contact
your smile
bat yuh eyelashes
mek im feel like a man
                but to the black man
         yuh nah even look at im direction
         wen yuh eyes meet his yuh scowl
              like im smell fowl
                but to the descendant of the Spaniard
                      the Portuguese
                the same who man the slave ship Jesus
                          yuh smile
                      im you show love
            but black woman is yuhself yuh hate
            is a hatred festering in yuh very soul
                      yuh nah to blame

I understand your father molest yuh
yuh brother molest yuh
yuh uncle molest yuh
dem have the same self-hatred in dem soul
dem nah whole
but that Spaniard that Portuguese
im nah just rape yuh yuh know?
Im sodomize you
Im dehumanize you
Im so tie yuh up like a darg
and beat you senseless
Im tek yuh pregnant
wit im bastard pikney
tie one leg to one horse
the other to another
then giddy up dem in opposite directions
and as yuh split in two
and the bastard fetus pops out
im laugh
        dis is the man yuh find it in yuh art to forgive
        dis is de man yuh say im good man
        but for every black man
        who gave into the illness of self-hate
        and visited the same on you
        two more fed you and clothed you
        protected you and loved you

but still you hate the Blackman
me say is yuh self yuh hate
yuh hate yuh father
yuh hate yu brother
so naturally yuh hate yuh mother
who took the seed of yuh father
and birthed yuh brother
is yuh self yuh hate
the black man is but
the manifested reflection
of the Blackman within you
so yuh can't hate him
without hating you
is not love you have
for that Spaniard yuh know?
Is spite yuh spiting the Blackman
who knows he is your protector
who knows you are his source of power
who will give his very life in exchange for yours
Is pain yuh feeling
So like misery you want company
you want me to feel yuh pain
but me sistah
I already do.

Haiku for Haiti

They hate you Haiti

You broke ranks dared to be free

I love you Haiti

Love is us

Behold the sun rising in the East
bringing the genius of a people
a people destined to lift the world
from doom and despair
with lifted minds
        we heal the wounds of burdened years
          a people gifted for reading signs
            dispelling fears
            a beautiful people
              while some ponder the meaning of life
                life is but the meaning love
              the silent pauses between heartbeats
                as blood rumbles thru the veins
                  echoes of rain
                falling thru the meridians
                  of time and space
           life and love are inseparable
           study then the mathematics of being
           where life is love and love is us
           who then can master us
           when love is the master of us all
the world is the very reflection
thru which the seeds of love are manifested
man and woman tested
as gods
defy the laws of the universe
        and curses rain down on heads of state
        a head waits states of mass confusion
        conclusion to a long and restless night
          provocations of thoughts thought of
          before time was
          behold the sun rising in the East

Scent from heaven

She is the essence of spiritual emanations
set in motion
with the utterance of Divine Algebraic Equations
she cannot be classified
with mere mundane characterizations
this manifestation of multi-dimensional
mathematical proportions
required verses
spun from metaphors
weaved into Spoken Words
unrehearsed songs sung in keys
that unlocked doors
wherein we find
the very hieroglyphical language
of the god-mind
she is Cleopatra
re-born from the sea of antiquity
seasoned with the virtues of social loyalty
'she loves blackmen'
long were the days men prayed
for the return of such royalty
prose of praises arose
in the form of ancient poetry
men meditated daily
on the source of her divinity
pushing beyond limitations
imposed by fear and learned subserviancy
to those men who came to know inner beauty
she is Nefatari
deeply enhanced
with a hue of mahogany
sun-sheened
with delicate hints of ebony

her eyes are like the stars
we gaze upon at night
twinkling with the very thoughts
thought of before time was
                              her lips
                       full and wet
flowed like a river of sweet nectar refined
              their parting revealed
        a definition of perfection designed
                 to activate
                 then satiate
           even the dullest of senses
mere men would say she smiled
                   but to me?
time stood still for a while
                           long enough to savor
           the sweet smell of her performances
                                to revel
in the deep well of her supreme 'for instances'
                            for instance
                   to inhale her mist
                      not in haste
                      but patiently
            for patience is a necessity
         to taste the very tears of god
                  her mere presence
       meant to chase the very fears
               from the hearts of men
        she is Heaven Scent to hell
           to give the very devil
     another chance to rise above
               she is Love

The Pros and Cons

In the beginning
it was all about revolution
reparations
free the land
then came the slam
The Def Jam
broke the body into fourteen pieces
everybody had to have their own band
do their own thang
open mic for sale
at every bar, restaurant, bookstore
seven at the door
raise a ruckus on the floor
and you just might be the next pro

convincing themselves
they be top dogs on these death rows
I suppose they propose the status quo of hoes
for they too claim to be pros you see
offering for a fee
what is free
to you and me

not for talent that sets them apart
save for the passing of the buck
see them drop to all fours
third eye closed
legs wide open
straight wishing for good luck

but luck has gone straight to hell
relegated to the realms of virtual reality
a mere man-made version of Divine destiny
for we be the gods that bless
and we be the gods that curse
so whosoever be the best
let them confess
that they be as good as the worse
for as much as they do unto the least
they do also unto the Most

Dreams and Scars

I beheld seven stars
aligned on her breast where her heartbeats
and in the seven stars I saw seven minds
each contemplating seven thoughts
in seven ways
each way having seven days

and on the seventh day of the seventh way
I beheld seven scars
scars that be holding inter-terrestrial energies
like burdens of past pains pent up

burdens burning with fire and brimstones
burdens of shattered dreams broken bones
bones of unknown ancestors
like Shaka and the Zulu dancers

those who tap danced on water
who can see into the future
and see the coming of the son
bringing fertility to she
who holds the seven stars for you
she who holds our dreams
our very meaning

that we be the dreamers of the seven stars
the dreamers with the seven scars
dreamers behind bars
for dreams are but scars
pressed upon the bars of time
as time unfolds into the future
taking with it a reminder of the past

The Wait Game

                                        He was moving weight
                                                to friend foe and kin
                                      said baby this dope game
                                                  I ain't really in
                                      pay off them high bills
                             so we can get back to living
                                        put paper aside
                       for when push comes to shoving
but he had his eyes on becoming king pin
got careless made mistakes
too many folks he was trusting
that's when the state came for him
she said she would wait for him
                            now he got her moving weight for him
                            he pushing up weight in the yard gym
                               she thought she had a man in him
                                         but a real man
                          won't make his woman sling for him
                                    her weakness was
                         she had more than a thing for him
feeling trapped by emotions emoting
the weight of the thought of leaving him
the thought of loving him
weighted down
by the thought of waiting for him
                     a two year stretch he's two years in
                             she's two months late
                             hungry all the time
                  and damn she's gaining weight

test positive
she feels negative
life growing inside
to live or not to live
she said she would wait for him
now she's pushing weight for him
everyday gaining weight cause of him
he wanted her to abort her weight gain
told her it was all about the weight game
but she refused to throw her life away for him
this life growing inside she won't throw away for him
now it's time she relieved herself of the weight of him
shrug that weight off her shoulders
exhale
and live life
for the life within
                              she said she would wait for him
                                    but the weight of him
                                        is a burden too heavy
                                            to carry for him
                                                this life inside
was the only weight worth carrying
and in the ninth month
on the ninth day
she gave birth
to him

Are you game?

They do not care why you make them feel superior to you
only that you do

They know that initially you are more than likely pretending
pretending that they are superior
in order to get that job
but now you must continue to pretend
in order to keep that job
to get that promotion
to keep that promotion

They know that if you keep pretending long enough
the deeper you will fall away from the real you
and soon
you will forget that you are pretending
you will really come to accept the lie
that they are superior to you

This is their game and they are the referees
you will not enter their ring and not fight their fight
not if you want to win at their game
so you will throw that punch
or you will be dis-qualified
you will throw that punch
with the intent to hurt your brother
or your brother who thinks he is your opponent
will hurt you first

You will be convinced that competition is your way
you will fight for that promotion
you will show initiative
(code word for playing dirty, snitching etc.)
you will try to outdo your brother
your sister
make a name for yourself
this is the American way
only the strong survives
you will show how strong you are
by crushing those in your way to success

You must win
so someone by default has to lose
but that's okay as long as it's not you
this is his game
this is not the African way

Whether we admit it to ourselves or not
we are all in his ring of death
whether you are a vendor on the streets
or a lawyer in the corporate towers
your only move is to survive long enough
to convince your opponent
that he is in fact your long lost brother
both of you working together
knock the referee to eff out
and end his reign of death matches
break the spell
are you game or gods?

Drops of Love

I long to be
these memories I see
memories of a black earth
giving birth
to ivory sands
fertile lands
acupunctured by tall trees
seas
teeming with life
in all varieties
indigenous nationalities
living in peace
within
these memories
I see

I long to be
what we used to be
masters of our destinies
High Priests and Priestesses
in perfect societies
socially responsible
economically viable
reliable
physically able
mentally stable
spiritually capable of making these memories
our reality

I long to be
but not to be
no less than what we can truly be

sowers of golden seeds
providers to each other's needs
reapers daily of bountiful harvests
keepers dearly of divine law
and the rain forests

these memories I see
and I know we can be
like king and queen again
I know we can reign
healing showers
for I feel my peoples' pain
I know we can rain
drops of love
til our cups runneth over
I know we can reign
life giving waters
to revitalize our earth
to cleanse her of the oil spills
the social ills
created by a race of people
in haste to taste
the fruits of the most high

these memories I see
for heaven's sake
and earth's too
we must reign, rain, reign
drops of love
again

__Let the children play__

Those once upon a time fairy tales
don't cut it no more
                it's time we rapped about
                    what's in store
                    hip, hop
                        if you think everything is hooray
                            then listen to the children
                            and what they have to say
                we are tired of dying
            at the hands of our brothers
                  tired of crying
            for the love of our mothers
      not knowing who our fathers are
            be they street vultures
                or behind bars
                why were we born
                  to die so soon
                  birthed at dawn
                  buried at noon?
here rests the body of young Jahson
shot by his brother's brother
there was no reason
may he rest in peace
until that day
when all Jah's children
raise their voices and say

to you brothers in the hood
stop killing us
to our mothers bad and good
be raising us
we need a place to play
where no drive-bys
we need a place to lay
where no bullets fly
as children we should be happy
not filled with sorrow
take good care of us
to ensure your tomorrow

Season of Tears

These moments I live
I give
and I take
but the more I give
the more I wake
consciously
I elevate

and like change become the seasons
I pursue other courses of reason
of course I reason
that I and the seasons
are one

like the new born that springs
into this world screaming
like the winds of march
blowing this way
then that way
and sometimes too harsh
these moments I have lived

I hear vibrations of rebirth
reverberating thru out
even the least of creation
re-breathing the breath of life
into a sleeping nation

listen to the babies cry
as Lazarus comes forth
listen to the March winds blow
bringing good news to the north
their sound is one

and soon the rains will come
as the sky becomes
like and open book
I look

I see him
giving all of himself
to the hungry earth below
filling her every crack and crevices
with all that he knows
listen to the babies
wail in the night

like the torrential downpour of possibilities
drawn to her undertow
where currents of potentialities
are waiting to birth new life
as moments of realities
these moments I live

as the cries of the babies
become sounds of laughter
tears are dried
under the heat of the sun
as the temperature climbs
higher and higher

these are the days
when the child goes out to play
some return home
some go astray
let the children play

for in each act of this play
they learn what to say
and when to say
we pray
they learn it well
this world can be like heaven
this world can be like hell

so thru scarred knees
and bruised elbows
the child grows
and with each fall
I realize
I am not All
I need another
to comeforth with me
not just the mother of all I see
for the father of all that I can be
but a lover like she

so I can be we
so we can be
two souls joined
together in perfect harmony
hearts beating each other's names
in splendid symphony
like the flutter of leaves
falling from the trees
these moments I live for
for the child is grown now
he plays no more
as the cold winter's air
calls him home now
he says no more
as he rests now
dreaming the spring

To be continued

How long shall we continue to do good
unto those who despitefully use us
abuse us

oh but to reap
the benefits of our labor
they do not choose us
like Mumia
they wrongfully accuse us
refuse us

our right to sit
on the front
or the back
the right hand
or the left
of our own throne
to self-determine
our own destiny
I ask how long
shall we continue

while the seeds they sow
grow
into weeds that strangle
yet do we echo their star spangle
the banner that goes
before the war heads
then presented
to mothers of the dead

our lives we pledge
to this symbol of perpetual enslavement
spiritual dismemberment
like many warring tribes
we come now like victims
of ill-temperaments
I ask how long

shall we continue to do good
unto those who despitefully use us
abuse us
accuse us
refuse us
shall we continue to be discontinued?
this question is to be continued
in your mind

The Beginning

'We do not risk the loss of self in love relationships because love is the natural state of being…it is not anxiety producing, It is natural'

Dr. Marimba Ani *'Yurugu'*

'The only hope for the kind of racial unity that will really liberate the Blacks in America and command the respect of the world will be a new kind of mass organization on a scale with an action program never before attempted'

Chancellor Williams '*The Destruction of Black Civilization'*

'If black male/black female alienation is not resolved, is there hope for a meaningful future for the Black race…Already some Blacks are discussing 'the relationship between the Black male and the white female' or 'the Black female and the white male' These discussions indicate that alienation has grown to the point of Black racial suicide.

Dr. Frances Cress Welsing *'The Isis Papers'*

'Furthermore the woman must be seen as the embodiment of the female aspect of God and the man as the masculine'

Ra Un Nefer *'Metu Neter vol. 1'*

'Love is the Inter-dependence between all things, it is the very fabric of creation, it is Maat'

Rudwaan

coming next
coming next
coming next
coming next
coming next
coming next
coming next
coming next
coming next
coming next

from this author

<u>The Next Test-of-men</u>

www.ingramcontent.com/pod-product-compliance
Lightning Source LLC
Chambersburg PA
CBHW070929160426
43193CB00011B/1619